Cry
Perfume

CRY PERFUME

Sadie Dupuis

Black Ocean
Boston · Chicago

Black Ocean
P.O. Box 52030
Boston, MA 02205
blackocean.org

Cover Art and Design by Julian Montague
Book Design by Anuj Mathur

ISBN: 9781939568625

Library of Congress Control Number: 2022933042

The text of *Cry Perfume* is set in Filson Pro and Goudy Old Style. Earlier versions of some of these poems were first published in *Blush Lit*, *Folkadelphia*, *Ghost Proposal*, *Hayden's Ferry Review*, *Hobart Pulp*, *Midst*, *Mutiny!*, *New South*, *On Loan from the Cosmos*, *Voicemail Poems*, and *Yes Poetry*.

FIRST EDITION

Contents

Black Number

FAKE BLOOD ON A FAKE FUR COAT

On a dark ride with my devious nature
What can I manifest, filling hole after hole
Blue flame for power
Black flame for tender
Days of uncleanliness patterned like a remedy
One gnat for the drinking glass
Dried onion on the stairs
It's the second month of the year and the second hour after midnight
Make your land uncomfortable if you really want to leave
But I really want to wait out the puffy endlessness
Hands in the holes in the satin pockets
Deep silk of uncharacteristic weather
Which never again changes
Only my ego, and it's splattered

PARKING FOR THE FUNERAL

One week later I'm a completely different person.
I don't even recognize the person from eight days ago.
Their unrelated habits and features, askew and sourer breath.
The one who bruised and scraped up
my undersides, that was a fleeting stranger.
Doing the work. We're doing the work. Working every day
to tolerate an airport breakfast, show up
at the gig without bloodshot anything, trot
past the bronze lion without haste.
Neck thick like a wolfman. It takes taming.
From the lightning sky, dead in the tongue.
Wrapped in a rainbow like always, divorcing myself.

CRYSTAL THINKING

Dream logic gets my sober companion drunk
Vomiting silver in the private beehive of our wagon
I went to the cemetery and played you a too-fast solo
Mud seeped in the ass of my off-black jeans
immobile on the morbid floor
Warmed last night with a controlled bedroom burn
just to plainly sing a song you danced to maybe
Time tape loops when I come here, abducts
even without crystal or crag
Gathering shells and birthday candles
I line them flush to you
Whispering love in skunk-hallowed territory
Poor me, but a possum only lives two years
Baby hyperventilating to his soothing music and cracked window
Trimming the crusts on my stories

CHATEAU MARMONT BUT FOR FREE

Diagnose me, interleaving
the peppers in my teeth.
I try to let lay my passive nature
but I need to get given the loot.
Hold cursed coins in my hair,
darn stockings from gold spiders
in the bungalow where I dreamed my master
piece and lost it over a morning's gallon.
Hammocks are for the purgatorial
swaying aspiration of suspense.
Neither here nor there but there
and for peanuts, closing
my throat as I swallow the world.

SHOUT OUT TO MY HEX

What do you owe the dead
When you know no one and are unknown
Making bridges
Making a metal fugue
Making a pastel binding

Police chase on the forbidden
Scanner as the ghouls skateboard
Past my window
A limo cuts them off
I know what you did last
Eternity in the golden whatever

My brain shuts down
At your closing credits
So much art I won't poke at
What do you listen to
Asks a manager next to me
At the raucous memorial
My dark holdings limited

Perfect awards show face when
My eulogy's in the window

WHITE DIAMOND

Curb the dog before
we're yanked into the other
diamond world. The mine
overglowed with glimmer
blocking hoof and wheel.
If something happens to me
release my sermons to the sand.
If something happens
keep whispering precious smoke.
Write out a blank note.
Shrink down in the rivulet
with palms wet. The dog
yanks toward the cascade
like did you see that?
Do you see? How loopy are we
to whoa out of paradise.

OUTREACH FROM AN OPEN WINDOW

There's that old bricklayer to seal me in again.
My acquaintance hops in and out of my life
regular as tongue fuzz.

With my bow and any number of arrows
every day is day
in and day seized.

The concept is opportunity
presents itself and I
should produce myself to it.
When the bricks settle
I blink at the pathway.

Flake that red rust.

The overlord tidies up
a speck at a time.

COME OVER MAKE MAC AND CHEESE :)

Do your love letters sustain you?
Salt the pot some time.

Playacting the protagonist for decades
gets you only decades past the start.

Pressurized in celluloid's single-use mania
wondering how any of us make it through
the soirée of end times grief.

You are rightfully cast as the accidental
+1 at a minor celebrity's private birthday.

Alone at a bar with your hero dead by death.
Winning bingo just makes your heart race.
Ruining your life by romantic candlelight.

Put on the magic glasses.
Confront the mirror.

STAR WARS IS FOR ME

because I know I'll never die.
The stalker sends me a video of me
while I sit cross-legged folding gorgeous silks.
These beautiful dresses I wish I wore
to beautiful activities, not fetal in a dog bed
simpering over a danger. Danger that won't
kill me because it can't. A gun in my evening
gloved-hands—couldn't be. Because we melted
all the guns and the cops' were the first.
Forge from the metal a ring of protection, invisible
steel against nightmares and curses.
The rictus I'll wear till I live.

YOUR SHIRT STILL SMELLS LIKE YOU

There was something
about living in the steadfast
city which opened
my eyes open.

Furniture stacked
like strange thrones.
A ceiling full of mold
and door crocked.

With a veil of skin
imagine just losing
a bulk of life.

Misery is real
so might as well chase it.
You tag along, antagonizing
a collection of sea-sore letters.

I don't look good in that
but it depends who's looking.
For a dress to zip in the back
requires a hand to hold it.

PALINDROME DAY

What's it like to just not be?
Million-and-one foot wave
drowned a blank passport.
Out of the undertow
two wet wires to solder.

Turtlenecks on stitched up stuffed together
corpse bits, spleen in catty clutches.

Harbor the cool for handshake tyranny.
On a tether, keep coming
back to the blue house, gutted.

It's really important to me
that it's really me too.
Me too, it's that important, really.
It's me, testatrix to the mud.

HI IT'S SAD

Sparkles of lime eke in recess pink
when no one wants you or no one
is hungry enough to want

Endless nosebleed was an omen
to give blood till you stopped eating it

Used two knuckles to hollow the bite marks
Silk robe swaying in the wind of devotion

Incarnate of the most corrupt talk show
came back an extra doomed diva

Please describe each every average
day as brutal, stock taken of each lie's good

Latch your floor at the neighbor's footsteps lo
Brain like an unlocked drum rumbling oblivion

The problem with votives
is you won't blow them out

HOLD PRESSER

you're the best you're beset
you've embezzled beelzebub
les legion legendarily tender
wary by design theoretical
under penalty of infrared
make the hair bigger
neck longer/thinner
the lips the red of the light
closer to the original painting
craning and cavorting
I don't like how I use
okay feelings about now I don't
really wanna you're bestial
a celebrity bezel philistine too
celestite progressing on overgrown
tiptoed squinches one of you two
is lying send the sideways
squareface to tease out the positive
additive adduct the calves depress
the scapula wellness is a rosy
tragicomedy see the party
jester's show in the sold-out morgue

SCREAMER

My night was real.
Its terror was real.
I pictured the killer.
Days later he killed
from the next night over
and over shouting
help me to the highway
7 pm in plain sight alleged
in the river and bubbles
stopped so they dragged it.
An animal scratches at the window.
Stretching over myself
pimples and ingrowns
bitterly tangled
hot vinegar burn and a
cracked spirit.
Couldn't she live
without the surprise.

DON'T SAY A WORD

In the afterlife you darn
like an automaton purring

A great heron flew alongside the lake
A sign of good to come
The most breeze in history, another sign

I don't have the brawn to ignore
signs from another species

Mend a prayer. Listen better
to purple at twilight

And ask to be sewn up
when each centimeter's fraying

STEAL MY SUNSHINE

Day one cancer season
sitting on the floor of a
blasting shower. Day two

cancer season fuck you
bring it. Picturing sunflowers
brains blanketing the coffins

this was a summer regular
another relic to the truck-chasing
dirty footed youth of greens toned

(dream, the kind after you've fallen
back asleep tense and vivid
impossibly vast for the minutes).

Writing your name in honey
on a slip of paper and hiding
that in a drawer for underwear

how much grief is normal?
What's normal is losing
so many hours to interstitial nightmares

waking, wanting
to commemorate forever
(falling off the balance beam)

into new methods of grieving
what's still here. I grieve,
I spend harrowing timelosses chewing

away the sides of my fingers imagining
a world without. Deprivation
bereavement bereft how much

is normal? My head between breasts
a chemical warmth, the security
of wallowing in an overcoat.

Night gave me ecstasy. This will ruin
our friendship, the wetness of death
through denim, normal? You can try

to normalize death like sunshine
cats babies birdbaths baggies
of power the bed loaned me

to be with someone I really loved.
I was over it while death
informed every swivel and suck-neck

saber-tongued tears of pride
as you fold into the web-grained darkness.
In the sunflower maze

following your broken trail
smoke in a smog.
With the spell in my pants pocket

delusional by necessity.
I want the month underwater.
Pruning, scaling, horning, eyes marquee

red full of darts wet at throat
the sight of monsters the gesture
of sharing my paw. You can set fire

to the surface of the water, alight every
river, block your passage to the openness
of the (salty) sea, destroy your way

but you aren't above love.
You always needed love.
You always needed love. You

always needed love you
were always parched.
Ready to be overcome

by love taxing
your bloodstream
your reign

you are ready to be
love to death.

Violet Noise

THERE'S NO AMERICAN BEACH YOU LIKE

I'm a troubled genius and that is why I need
the ice cream. Melting down in the bathroom
after falling on accident into her nudes.
Molten me slides down the drain and comes
up another shower, the surprise attack
you replay so often it splits the universe.
Just a regular monster with many sick beats.
I take braids from she who shouldn't.
I build a nest of small fingernails.
It is a prudish and puritanical nest, that's not the same
as pure but I am. Listen to my brilliant beat!
Mottled by cavity, marbled by overgrowth,
crusted in the bleached sugar I take to sleep.

CRACK MY BACK

The money's in fiction
I can handle the truth
I came back from the horror
Where someone's in the backseat
Worldbuilding my whole mental state
When I look in the rearview
Mirror I am that bitch
Back in hell again
Wondering how to drink
Less without quitting
You were as beautiful
As an infant rabbit
Orphaned and shaking in the march
Chrysanthemum mist
Waiting in the women's room but why?
It's strange to remember your past lives
Only three years ago I was coolest
And therefore the worst because you knew me
When I had no confidence and I still don't
The shytown starlet sinks to the bottom
Retrieving the lost ring
Proposal as penance for roughhousing
A lovely spine I could snap with my thumb
Romcom people love each other I love

Making a mess of my things
Losing gloves 10 minutes into buying them
And treating friends like customers
I could've been married by now I was
Confessing in the toilet stall
You'll always be underage to me
At the children's table
Reciting a mutilants' valentine
Prince Valiant depressed because he stopped
Reading 20 books piled under his ass
The princess and the acquisitional fetishism
Is there a political point to naming
Your friends at dinner feeling like a starfucker
Feeling like your favorite B and C cities are
An obsession with America
Imagined without the Ks
Get out of the industry
Pursue your pilot's license
Speak into phones with foxy kitten coos
Mental toughness is what the fuck I'm talking about
Cream blush on the face of a cockroach
Brow pomade spreading the staph
He's never heard someone talk about lipstick so much
I think he ought to wear it now
It's good to stumble with your breath
I can never embarrass myself again without
Quitting air

VIEW-MASTER CLASSIC

The monster lands in front of us
Amorphous smoke billowing
Facade of swollen snow

Genius is like this
The meaning in its kiss
Encrypted with broken desire

A story of offscreen fame

A soundalike for fantasy
Insufficiently perfect
Repeating the chain link

Telepathy's in duplication
Touch the psychic body

No, like this

OH GOD I JUST WATCHED A MAN

set different metals on fire and that was his whole "set."
Moreover I've seen him do it all before!
I'll never be alone, too many people
do it badly and I'm too self-ashamed to do bad.
Books > "music" because no one ever reads
40 minutes of fire. I'm just trying
to drunk mind-meld with my online friends
order a cinnamon cocktail and live
through the snow squalls, unobtrusive
thoughts on constant flame. Crop top
in the chimney flue, burning
marshmallows in honor of the dead
famous drummer. Some day I'll jiggle
my feet so fast I flare. Earlier this other
customer said don't you come in here
with your kid? My kid! I cackled! There's no kid!
And there never will be! And that! Was my solo set!

MOST BEAUTIFUL SNAIL OF DISNEYLAND

I'm out of my elegance
dressed in scalding water
while the old guard smokes noisily
outside my bedside.
You've held this job two thousand years
now I'm here to replace you.
I don't smell like you
so all manner of flora flock
to me. I wish we
all could be cloaked
in this ancient seaweed.
You, 2000, me, 33, all of us
modular bodies in between.
Hermit crabs trading homes
borrowed or thieved
in methodical order.

ANAHEIM WITHOUT SUN

These I keep and these I can't
Cactus doesn't bloom there
Played chess with a Caravaggio type
Then picnicked a lot
So the sunglasses don't yet come off
I have that coping inside
Synths enter my head—
what, because they can?
Bull giving up
Got the whole world headbutting
Festivals are the end
of a sense of a sense of a party
I demo them dead

THE LANCE GOES THROUGH

I started crying to songs that made me cry
Piling boulders atop my fretful parts

Every night it's night again
Every morning is a rune

And now there's a stain and all day
I've showed it off for the right people

In raspberry tulle wielding a kitchen knife
Dial my phone to finish the riddle

The difference between mania and ringing a bell
Only one makes me make bad wishes

LIMERANCE

When someone emails on stage
Asking me out of my way
As if fate didn't schedule the annoyance
Replying is never a must

Me up to my that's-so-me
Cede the crowd
The clearing of viscera

Why his band and not me
Fucking around instead of standing
Drink in the request
Music guards the opening night

BOWLING A 666

Today I saw the best show ever.
Today I drank the best tonic, it was bought for me.

My ambition keeps me fixed to the pratly center part
of a guitarist with no dynamics.

Friday the 10th and it's not auspicious.
In the mint washroom with yellowed egg wall prints
constructing a mental self-portrait for a lineup of pinups.

Reprieve from the machismo of excessive quiet.
The anxiousness of sitting on a stool without purpose
dying for the real agenda to blast up and away.

Staid out on my ass as the boredom
chords wash out and in.

It isn't my choice if the work transfigures.
The arrangements spat out of the stars.

NAMES CHANGED

I don't think I'm famous except for when you think I'm famous.
Am I your most famous you fucked?
My friends' friend's ex fucked POWERLINE.
Technically it was a cheating.
They said their sale was sold for fame
still I buy two booze and feel glad
exes get exed if I become new.
Since you want my chart you conclude
I mark my feuds as pick-me-ups.
The stars in poems? Sorry but that's over now.
When I'm cursed into eternal slumber
the bad boy faces the fax.
Turn it around and smother
with sacred slather.
You run and you hide.
You delete your own mind.
I'm always my most famous one. Fucked.

TEN MINUTE SET TIME

My man can't watch the murder
shows with me, he gets too queasy
seeing from a fiendish perspective

Meantime, get ready for this loser shift
Crawling out under the lectern
after his millionth tepid word

Coolness sleeps growling at my feet
The crowd vacates its bodies, gazing for exits
retreating to burned-out fantasy cellars

Casket sized luggage overstuffed
with fake flowers while the long-winded
improviser queued up gurgles of vacuums

Interminably time-wasting

When you drag out your language you flip inward
The more you perform
the quieter you become

AND THIS MAN DOESN'T WANT TO MAKE
MUSIC WITH ME

because I hate the corporation. The corporation
which built the spatters, slatterns,
bars across the sky. The corporation
which goads us to blink less, float glumly and night
terror through the hallways of another
posey-closed chain. The corporateer
injecting a poison thus in my mandible,
the corporate memo advising me I'm not
hot but should be, not in the way
of glitter and slits but a farce
formed of playplace elastica. The corporate board
tucking me in at night. Another decade of loving
CFO and CTO. Awake, shaken, gazing a hole.
Making music alone—I hated it back.

MAY THE BODYSNATCH KICK IN

It's you and me baby
in the hospital hot tub
waiting out the weekend ordeal

Pizzazz and a pair of headphones
up to our stents in mailorder sulphur

Turns out I write
very special words

Here's an apology dictation:
sorry
I'm lost
in the color blocks
of a digital map
of the woods of inferno
begging my second wind
naked without context
scared to change routes
and sorry

One more volcanic world on my plate
apart from the one we stew in

MY SATURNALIA

The betrothed ascending
the never bending stairs
leaves behind her curlicue ribbon

I don't know how long I can stay
aggressively ugly in my devotion
to the staring contest, jaw locked
down in a vat of burgundy

*
**

Scouts in the woods and side to side
walking off the matte horizon submerge
when the flight stops upon a gulf

I take her hand from the river's bottom
Swimming under the rhythmic current
Sometimes life really is a storybook
In that case we better cheer up soon

*
**

Feet upright tap dancing in space
It's normal to do it on your back

If I hook it on a line, the bait
doesn't graze the pond's surface
Identical voices winding into one
twine of melancholic tremors

*
* *

The first lost boy I remember
stole me Pop-Tarts in the cafeteria
Partying alone whenever he never
came back. I sure took my share of pain

pills when they gave me two months'
Stop dancing so fast
Your world is bigger than that

*
* *

Everything is handsome enough
in tie-dye wash

Ego in amateurs, mastery
in abstraction, laughter after
esteem, kindness in slaughter,
lengthy origin stories,
engagements without questions

Parts of life just aren't beautiful

* * *

Stamina tires
when the night rounds up

Drying the men's clothes
on a string looped loosely
to the back end of a trailer

* * *

Flagging down the fast way
whoever you were
through dust and gravel

I love to feel the bass
with way too many little notes
I make a promise
to vanish the world

*
**

The poet is the sibling of the singer
I learned right after I learned
the poet is too poet here

I don't review art
When I like it I like it
embarrassingly,
I can't hide my face in words

*
**

Smashing pedestrians as adrenal feeder
Slowdance with the broom to a twinkle
Sneering and hiccoughing in the eyes of love

Am I better
writing because I write
Because I write music I am making it all worse

*
**

Because I write clinical music

Those octave shifts are the find of my life
The FM amble propped me when I was bare
Drums made whole from a bajillion ickle bitties

*
**

She put her voice underwater
She cast her voice to a distant planet

The corner of her eye projects her starved yearning
Ecstasy melting in this model schema
Surreptitious players pretend they have it worst

*
**

The last time I couldn't work I worked
on learning every song by your old band

My tendons wilted at this venture
We were a pretty solid group
forearms and fingers and thumb

I'm going there, pneumonic
father of the fathered
past the paint of mentorship

Sitting in steam
together you spill all over
the seam where we might combine
an odd edge with a nice notion

Tears well in my memory
Dry red face coming back alive
Lying on the carpet in love with sound

My voice stretches out to atmosphere
It circles the cemetery gates
the hillside daffodils
the cyclists whizzing lazily
the families in my mouth

Sings of mixed-up hearts
Frowning by the poolside

Glaring in the ice cream parlor
Scowling to my waltz steps

Glowering at the casino
Daggers for my near love

With my eyes shut, I made it from point A
to another point in the solar system

Death stares on the pleasure wheel
My face is feeling up my fate
Kisses all the way up

Green Spell

MY PRETTY POET

I chew up my feet
Running down a mountain times five
When I buy the green gem
I'm envied by thousands
When I look into the makeup monitor
My eyes are the color of American money
Bleach-sanitized

There are two rescue seals
And I squat naked in front of a curtain
Legs spread like a man at work
At work against the demons in my molar
Which pummel each other all through the nights
Waiting to pop out my skull
Surprise
You were bad all along
The only pretty thing in this evil world
Is the ghastly bitch

ONE SITE POSTS TO THE OTHER

It's not cathartic crying on an exercise machine
just a bright migraine I self-induce.

Bees in the gag now. Snotting into escrow.

Each day my face is unrecognizable to me
making it hard to establish a cosmetic practice.

Tried to get into myself so much I locked me out.
Beautified, a draconian tag that needs to get low.

I die by the record and un-die.
If the DJ plays my song I crown them queen.

If the DJ spots me in the crowd they know before I do
whether my mask is really this scary.

LOL

Deftly I network
out of the thrum
to my phantom subterranea

Promos hovering
lo like bats
the flying dream
where you frantically paddle
your claws off the porn

Do you still want
to be my duplicate

Does my voice offer
a genial uncanny

So glum all twisted
in a slipshod knot

It's me conning my way into the gleaming credentials
vs me who can't just go buy a new one

TRANSLATION OWN

The reviews are out: blaaaaaaaaaaaaaaaaaaaaaaaaarrrrrrrrrrrgh.
What do I make of that?
Dragons invaded the wrong land.
You're coming home with me
asked the nemesis, stating it.

I became baroque to fake ownership
of a body estranged from its brain.
Drink some water. Take a walk.
Pretend to have some claim to water.

Blackmailer in the polar night
glues down a giggly ode.
I'm bound to these drab and hollow nouns.

FREEFALL THROUGH A BLACK HOLE

What happens in this movie is the story of my life.
There are too many paths to disaster, that's why every inch aches.
He lies on top, juicing me down to jetsam.

In the family flower shop but every plant is wilting.
In the checkout candy corner every candy is plain.
Showed up for our date in my carnival clothes.

The nature of my work is to be crushed beneath a paperweight.
Argent morning, trace a line with a board game wand.

The sieve of myself I sift
through as I see myself out.

A door closes, a door closes, a door closes.
Put a foot in the frame already.

I TRIED ALL THE FREE TRIALS

Now there's nothing left to do.
I bit a little bite of each cookie
then they cut me off.
Your foe brought me a cavalier breath.
Sip of ice, an immense strain.
Simpering for the cherry blossoms, it costs nothing.
I influence myself to make fabulous future purchases.
Like opening a fifth account.
Dangling from it.
There are consequences, also free.

HORSE HAVEN ROAD

I declined to give my interview
atop the mound of sputum.
Why not highlight the sputum itself
I asked the reporter, sinking down
my gelatinous platform.
Schmoozing it up in the cytoplasm
I passed on the unpaid opportunity
to make marvels from this sick.
I cleared space for the gunk
and slime to enter me
to speak through me
to fill me up so huge
everyone would be forced to stare
at the goop-stuffed husk.
We charged five bucks for a mucosal postcard.
Ten for a kiss caked in bile.
This is how we grow the warmblood mountain.
Horses don't have these concerns.

THE THIRD PLACE

I unliked this so I could like it again
Frozen dew pocks my cheeks, icehead
Return to practice with dedication though do it languorous
Not everyone has access to the freshness you know

Sooo proud of you but
What role does justice play in your world
You were born in a castle of plastic
Is this whole life a mood
Plastic cup lids top the turrets
Plastic straws guide the drawbridge

Amazing
I love it
Wow nice
From the take-out container moat
Etching aspirations in the waste
The queen of the polyvinyl dump

FIGURE FOUR

With purpose I online myself
oily cheeks and hairs akimbo
so she texted me right away.

Miscalculate everyone's name
in the wrong state in new hair.
Curating treasures in a heap
of petticoat lamé.
So killingly crownable,
always doing the right thing first.

I'm very, very,
very, very, very
very pretty says
the greeting card.

My husband is doing the dishes.
My body lies over the sea.

FIRST TIME CALLER

Defeat the replies
Leave the junior room
You finally caught the ominous
and sideline your strangeness
Its size remains my fear
When the formant invades
Determined, alien, silver-mouthed
Satyr behind the lunar screen

Your beau makes legendary vows
I let the kid speak for me
While the lookout continues
Banded to the phantom city
Where scampering streets meet the big moon

Unilaterally astronomers predict
Earths are trembling
Golf claps to high heaven
Viscous mirage revealing you
Suddenly, who must be new

WATCHING STREAMING WITH MY
MARRIED FRIENDS

The enemy of my enemy is my celebrity crush
The wife of my enemy won't canoodle
I know some guys who go by Ron
Never accused of hiding behind an assumed name
They have never been doxxed
Why is it when men excel
Well why do they
A method golden
In a field unlockable
Their way becomes pretty good
Don't sound like riot
Don't sound like brat
Don't sound like mother don't sound
like anyone except gladiators
longknifing off the wrinkles of Pioneertown
There's a purple kind of flower associated with fading
scented and blooming I can't remember the names
of flowers I was found in the field
ten feet beneath the permafrost

INVOICING

Hell is finical
Life is sponsored
I curse her on lunch hour
I don't want to get up and go go go
The sick, the sad, the strange
Take every corner of my crawly core
Live in the shell of piles

For a slow cab home in the soggy rain
For depression food delivered to the wrong door
For paths that are livable, none
For rent of the couch covers hourly

Developing the app that identifies magic stones
How many magic stones till I shed my imbalance?
$1, $10, $1,000,000,000,000,000,000
More like zero zero
zero zero zero zero

ASDFGHJKL

The grown fairy gifts practical jokes
A scalding honeybee soak
10 gallons of spewed wastewater

Needles in the task app
Framing my payment
methods that double as familiars

And you just left it under a pillow

CONGENITAL SUNBURN

Let's watch the movie
Then the documentary about the movie
Then the sequel to the documentary

Swaddled up in quilts
A dangerous baby animal
Can't get to its teeth

High-fiving from adjacent rollercoasters
We hold the other's hand
Butterflies as far
As each eye can trust

ERIC

I enter the conference call
and pretend I'm half my age
hometown boy sports star
from a matrilineal coven
in a town unlike our towns
where the cafés and cybercafés
say pray away catastrophe

I like the name Eric
I like to be a leading man
on the verge of crash
while reality resembles
the space beside a synapse
a hallucinated permanence or
grasping air and
touching it

THE GREAT OUTDOER

A hologram trims my dead
A robot performs my adjustment
A simulacrum dissolves me
While a cyborg doles out the antidote
One screen reads tea and the other
Screen exercises jowls, wattles
My girlfriend syncs to blue
Multi-monitoring while the wet world
Moans in lieu of a westernmost window
Immersion panel with HD scratch and sniff sunset

CATS WAS NOT REALISTIC

The wasteland doesn't
show her belly button,
its own minefield.
Scratch in the paint like
none of these cats napped.

REMARKABLE PIG

Good morning malaise.
The seawater rushes out my orifice.
The longing dries up in a pill of sand.

HOT TO DEATH

Ghost face is gone
with the hook-handed
7 days till ascension
Heart in my gullet
Admire the put upon
Jumps that washed up
Grimace and grin contorted
A simple mask unlifted
Keeping you you while you
Crawl around the ceiling
Entrailsing expertly
You fade into view
From the dark corner of a room
To never know you
Hot hot hot

ARE YOU DEALING WITH MORE STRESS

At sunrise arriving with every light on
and my face in the phone I felt dreams
withering, sweet sap wrung out in glitch.

It's not encouraging to make
someone laugh this hard at not-a-joke.

Were you penetrated by evil?
asked the warm spastic twitch.
No I just got worse
at dealing with it.

Today I saw a strong
aura after staring
at the ceiling, watermelon
ballooning green with a meat
pink middle blocking
out anyone's face.

There was too much
tedium in the cortex.
Every part of me is flashy.

So I make a bed for no one.
It's my golden birthday.

Red Arsenic

CODEINE RUSE

Here's a way of solving problems:
spit some stranger's life up
now cry perfume.

I shingle myself
pricking a square.

My commune shudders again
a loose key fallen from a ring.

Sardine censure
as our dancehalls keel.

I'M SO TIRED BY THE BEATLES

Drinking blood to stay awake
How much human stuff can you take?
Seventeen takes and minimally enrolled
in the real world. I was googling
where to get Narcan and instead
popped up on biodegradable highlight
Men tell me to keep writing
Well if you insist
What's a good word
to chuck here, an obscure word
An allegory for searching for myself
in online images as proof
of ID at the post office
When I fail to see through
the safeguards, 3D glasses on,
the spirits come without a prescription
Be there in the small town mill buildings
My black and white movie dreams
Show up because life is dotty
It's all anyone can do
Wired on plasma
into the mirror
I'm tired of you

BETA BLOCKER

Staving off humility
I suddenly sensed the wraith
behind the shut bedroom.
My esophagus sank
right into my asshole.
What formal message does a ghoul
send standing invisible, flowing
outside the fiction of my quarter?
Jerking under the fuschia disguise of time.
A tomorrow without possibility.
A fatalism I deny under penalty.
Shadow I step in, as it's mine.

NOBODY STRENGTH

Got home drenched
in repulsive throb
stripped the soiled shag
to a million stripes

I'm trying to show you
my impression of you
Soaking over the precipice

Be mine but be
away from me

The mark of comedy
What makes the oil essential
I anoint you in memory

A gesture I reflect
while I copy its everything

SATAN'S BIRTHDAY

Jab that elbow right in the killspot to relax
doing 120 on the border farm-to-market
rankling the tawny cats. It's a June-hot January
celebrating Satan's birthday at the cigarette deli.
Today he burns your favorite
band's best disc, trading necklaces like dogs
understudying your worst part
in the play. Chaotic chaotic.
Taffy stilettos and a cloven embrace.
The devil drinks the juice of a cucumber.

SAME NAME HEAD WOUND

Are you supposed to share your psychic dreams
or does telling them jinx them? The best parts of my life
are sad and silent, buying the night's last drink.

The obvious interpretation is I love you
bleeding in on my birthright carpet
telling jokes to keep conscious.

Pale memories mime a dance they do
clumsy. You're up early.
Kick your feet on the empty chair.

GIRL WHO IGNORES ME

You're not to let two days
get away from you, white petals
floating in the dirty slate bath.
Follow the bus to the pharmacopeia.
Incantatory saline, unseeable salve,
all so young so sick. White petals
circumnavigate the empty seethe.
There's not much time to find
a dare. White petals raining
from the ceiling. From the kites.
White petal crown.
Ignite.

OPENING CEREMONY CLOSING

Dropping my flies
in your outbox

I can't quit dousing
the alley in turpentine

when in mindful hindsight
I treated the villain charitably.

Projecting a superantihero
signal I salivate straight and pedantic
down canyons, over parapets.

You were sharing the magazine's back cover
regardless, sunny, sated

ready to count
the rings and to lay
a chemical trail.

Everyone working the steps.
Everyone working the room.

I've got one hand in your pocket
and I'm wringing out everything loud.

YOUR MICRODOSE

Fall behind the futuristic
infinitely more scuffed
Into my stein distribute
two vials of rose potion
99 wines dropped A lot
of strangers seem happy
not seeping the sun
Even in the sucky circumscription
Cute little stomach gamble
exing out boxes daily
for emotional alightness
Shoulder pads
Phony movements
Stringent copyright
chokeholds the clown
All my life
I loved a stuffed bear

LETTER TO MY ACOLYTE

Crawling from the k-hole
you oughta know
who's your best friend and why
you're sitting where you are at her wedding

Countless detours later
I loop the old scraping
scape into a fried throat
summonable only in exhaustion

I can't fake ballet the way I used to
hunkering down in first position
She pushed me against her hedge
covered my mouth a palmful

Moralistic river walk in soleless slippers
Merit badge please for my burst bluster

Rug burn all over from hugging someone stagnant

I miss my sister I have no sister
I love my sister I need my sister
Fuck my sister Grab my arms for support

At your convenience come and dismember
Phases stretched everywhere
Epistolary lucky charm

BRAIN SHANK

I hope it's a long nap
imagining comebacks
to newsworthy evil
that doesn't hit back

Dry nausea from the medical
office's carbon fountain
hitting arbitrary deadlines
you arbitrarily refused
my earnest request
to arbitrarily extend

This is the same
building as yesterday
the same place with no
bathroom so I don't drink

It's final boss after boss
after boss after boss
until someday you scratch
my scalp, pet my ponytail,
tuck me in forcibly
hire me to sleep

I THINK YOU JUST CALLED ME

Obsessed:

with an airport in the record
breaking winter heat with dry
cleaning the wrong
size white spaceship
purchased at discount as
retail perishes;

with buying another
car although urbanist
teens endorsed my
car with earning credit
for the thousand pots
of make-up anti-capitalist;

with this imaginary
feminist pro-harm
reduction sex
worker advocate cop
in this small
town crime procedural
ACAB with garlic
tea and wet sock

therapy as I scrolllllllll
past midnight;

with meeting a friendly
ghost but like only
in the daytime with
a royal ghost that lies
beside me warmly and fills
my mornings with hope

Obsessed with
my lies with me
King No One

THANKING THE CLOUDS

My true love sent me love
letters about a famous assault.

"Teamster," that's just a perfect word.

Humidity smacks the face
out of rain or fog.

In his too small
brown blazer remembering
icons who wane
in their comfortable chairs
autonomous chimes
in stormless rooms.

NAH

When a celebrity dies
I take a nap

Pardon me on my fourth
cup of poison

Saying fire your idiot
from his floating phone booth

Shifting black bismuth in the rental warship
The nag ends my mystical life

What I've done all day
What I'll do for the rest of time
So beautiful I snooze
Little finger on the needle

BULLDOG ME IN SALTED WATER

Frogs choose you as god then follow for life
Puffing over quick steps in cold ocean

Cloud scattered cigar ash all over the sea
A musk I draped in as the fake leader

It's me, you know me, you know what I'm like
Me in the sweaty palm of your permanent gripe

Jaws on the chew, chaff disregarded
Little bitch barking at the pearl of the world

WEIRD TOUCH I SPAT AS SHE SPIDERED

Two fingers from my shoulder
to my shoulder. Women also do weird
touch. But it's friends now okay okay
in the gross scheme of not wanting
at all to feel a friend. We're real friends
who talk on the phone. Vouch for me
ventricles. All hands on anonymous
musculature full of soap. Superficial but safe.
Gimme aloneness.

Blue Hour

FULL WORM MOON

Why not a cotton moon
Why not a work moon

Maybe it's a moon
startling me with itineraries

What should have been done at the last moon
What I hope to flower before the next

Moon like a razor, moon like a gutting, moon
that asks how your day was
Moon mailing the bouquets

Crawling around the belly
of the belle of the banquet

Moon settling down
in a house from which
it was evicted

Moon that supports you
down in the mud
twisting your back

Moon that slithers,
bisects, transforms

The transient way you wish
to phase across the atmosphere

INFERNAL CATALOG

Woke up with my head propped on a headache
I keep making appointments on the wrong holy day
Trolley tremors enrapture me like a cheat code
I never turn on the train without training tracks
Driving to nostalgic songs, nostalgic for nostalgia years
From across the aisle he screams he doesn't want to start an altercation
Shake a little steam out, things look grainier now
Green distorted to grey
Knitting and gripped to a government shopping spree
Spent hours on art of primacy before the software crashed
Starry colors hooting at minor maladies
At least you think of me when a song is strange

LAST NIGHT WAS MY NIGHT

Tonight as you superimpose your outfit on my
Outfit you superimpose your face on my face
You superimposition world wide open busted

It is burden to create so much
Ache in the crick wherever a crick can go
Why I oughta be crushed under stone

Processed molten mutable drying
In the mold I could be your body
For you I could eat lunch and immediately
Eat the second lunch

Off the back of your shape
Curved little uncontrollable
The one I came to hatch

GETAWAY CAR WITH A BILLIONAIRE

Unsuccessful and lonely
So imagine what it's like to go platinum
I rehearse the breakfast where we become true confidantes
Americana phonings exchanged
Overgrowth tallied on whitewall pencil
You're supposed to change your bath towels once in a while
And probably this mattress after sixteen soggy years
I had to be told
On my stomach with next week's leaves
Skimming and clucking like you'll all feel so sorry
When I'm a hit but who's you all in this reversal of fortune
Where my vague words wound archaic figments
I had to be told
The voices you trade for the voices you trade
For the hum of the heater at the peak of the dark
When my doorbell rings, I'm reduced to palpitations
Rehearsal of cordons from the unattended slay squabbling
Shepherding dust in its hovel of a home
Make a new fast friend every empty day

SMART ENOUGH TO PLAY ALONG

Versus too smart to even try
Lighting a fire under my asinine
Fantasy tutorial in pose and cologne
Auctioneer to shivering devotees
Now I'm looking in, now I'm looking not
Tell me your standardized scores
Extra ice in that cold cold water
When all you wanted was to be sober
Trees yanked out so they put them back in
No hindrance whatsoever to the flattening flack
A bird at the window keeps his neck on straight
Real girl in the world who would love to see you
Taking shots at the deeply dark
The bird at the window just warbled and lived

EUCALYPTUS PAYCHECK

Resources depleted but
you gotta get over the moat.
It was better the first time
with a maxed-out inner glow.
We're out of effigies
so I sport the signature cap of inheritance.
Bubbling up with my divining ram.
The source of my power
is my hairy big toe.
The source of my sadness
is when everyone fissures.
I'm from the big city, I only
need a pill and I was born
to impersonate. The chlorophyll
runs infinite in your private stream.
Beyond the pearlescent scantron
I really think you should pay more
to keep the stolen spoils yours.
At the crest of a parted waterfall
let your heart lead the crushing
crisp smell of a plant you extincted.

YES TEARS LEFT TO CRY

Peel me off the water
Shallow end lurching
With a nimble stiff

Tell me your favorite bad writers
Tell me about a woman who is
obsessed with if she is

Tell how talking about greatness
makes you less near the great

I follow the detective out to the pool
Against the radius clause
circling over the spot
where the dirt disappears

The skeezy speech of my old rival
sputters out without any say

I'm only men when it rains

FUCK NO TO ALL THAT

I'm not adventurous in my work today.
I'm not diving into the skin of horrors.

You cross Saturn
and parts of public life just die.

The little painful pull
—that's what age I'm at.

Naming names is a tack
to a time and place.

Wouldn't you like to transcend
time and place?

Finally I'm the classroom elder.
I imagine my cockcertainty shaking the querier.

Overpracticing a video girl
home routine with sedentary mind.

Popping hip out from throne,
giving mussy notes.

Reconnect the severed line
between brain and hand,

cut me out
of the slick photo.

BE MY VALENTINE II

Whatever white-knuckling means I just did it.
Revealed my intrinsic quality to myself:
knowing there's a blizzard, driving anyway.

And laughing out my teeth grindings.

Calm down to a clean chaos, the hypnosis
succumbed to in storms, 20 out of 10 stars. Walk me

to the gas station for a super big cup. Warm me
in your protection. I'm so buff when indignant,
tailing after an impervious emergency.

Ideal conditions in the gingerbread netherworld:
mediocre degrees out, dead tree skyline.
Acute grey changes that jaundice the lover.

TRAIN TRUNDLING, HARES NICKERING

I KNOW you took my top sheet off on PURPOSE
that is SUCH a BOY thing. I spray the flower water
with my mouth FULL of allergies, lip blistering,
quartz-soaked on linens, WRISTS, pulse of neck.
My wrists always rolling, to loll them NEVERENDING.
Labor in every LABORIOUS surge of the blood.
I am TRYING to make this life one uninterrupted shot
of an hourlong DREAM. Spotlight from the street lamp
SPITS into my teeth. Kiss me QUICK for eleven years.
Whether our team WINS or LOSES, it's FIREWORKS.

OH MY GOD SHOES

Wonder what it's like not to hear the bomb
Five left before the infrastructure collapse
My cradled egg experiment

Don't wear that sweet scent just to placate me
Spent red rose overcooking on the dashboard
Then dusting in the vase of my work boots

Who are you? That's my favorite question
When it's said in awe
When I've escaped or when I'm caught

Projecting my essence to an empty ballroom
Six static steps to believing in others
Tripping the lights in a closed-down arcade

So trained and capable I broke down in a rash
Boiling down others, aspiring to their innards
with double digits blades in my back

The way I'm appealing is appearing upside down
An hourglass in reverse, sandcastling
If you want a job done you must bring you your flowers

HOSTAGE SITUATION

These are simple demands I need followed.
Exceptional rules for the anthropomorphic heart.
Stick out my tongue so you read my past lives
and witness the generational sticktoitiveness
that dominates my origin story.
I can't write romance, I'm too busy
full-time filing my way through.
I can't write fantasy, I'm too stuck
waiting on the new paying off
the last, not just the subway to next week.
I can't write memoir, I'm scared
the men in my life will see themselves.
I can't write politics.

I can't write politics.
I can't write politics.

AMATEUR HONOR

Leading man stalks
through the one horse

shopping cart full of intuition
boosters, sopping

gal pals up with bland bread
The fireplace wouldn't turn

Blinking raccoon
reflecting off the one lamp

I find the embarrassment
marked with a streak of beige

Ice melts over
slipping with a plastic flute

He wants to plunge through,
jaw of a glacier

Last barn painted
like the first one

COME BACK AND PAY FOR THAT

Ask me anything about love.
I proffer a lie or evasion.

You're out in that weather
sourcing a replacement
when I already have a double!

Marked my place in my book
with a map of my city.
The ritual commences.

Some triangles point up.
It's enough for me to worry
myself awake when the bugs do.

MORNING HAS GOLD IN ITS MOUTH

Don't wear new chiffon
to feed the swamp flamingos
a voice shouted across the dull bog.

Buttoning instead
my tuxedo for bed.

There I wait for a pauper's kiss
from my still-jinxed prince.

He scoured my old notebooks
with a moldy talon and clattered
the virgin. I flew about an inch into the sun.

It was right to cheer for odd numbers.
To put aside my frilly fatality.
It was right to be trampled
in my dusty uniform.

Fist full of seed
for the very big bird.

SEEKING SWORDS

Awaken, county.
The surrounding hill
towns all with charming
fairy names: Airy
and Cinnamon, Ripple and Rose.

The place you fantasize
tying on the apron
is just four likely walls.

Slice your way through the cake
at a strong angle. When you zoom out
every escape route is wrapped
in an even bigger box.

10 AM CANYON

Tomorrow is consoling
all the way. Make me
feign fawning over another aquatic
posture. Go on snuff

the cobwebs off an antique. I live
my curiosity like the checkerboard, acquiring
au courant trinkets, shelling out
over a jar of backyard.

From a name on a mailbox I found
the celebrated's anonymity disowned,

namesake forewent, mitzvah,
obituary askance
with the usual creeping—

"last name gift registry"
"last name open casket"
"last name net worth."

Here is your PR: publish or punish.
Pose off the suburban line,
marzipan drapes drawn.
Payment for permission
to write this poem is
I had to pretend to be nice.

THE MOON ORDAINS

I should write my body night and day
Under the poorman's weatherglass
I just don't know how to lour
Tripping on a thousand new miles
It should be my work to drive at dark
To shovel the snowfall, to cover cooked rice
Before morning, swell with the sea
She should only think of me born smiling

Acknowledgments

Thanks to Dorothea Lasky, Wendy Xu and Caroline Crew for their generous guidance and perspective on the earliest drafts of this book. Thank you to Geoff Rickly, William Hutson and Rachel Syme for chaperoning me into the perfume blogosphere, which helped me dub this book's sections.

Thank you Janaka Stucky, Carrie Adams, Andie Sheridan, Charlotte Renner and the rest of Black Ocean & Chapter House for bringing *Cry Perfume* into the world. Thank you to Stephen Malkmus, Hanif Abdurraqib, Jenny Zhang, Brandon Stosuy, Eileen Myles, and Wendy Xu (agan! and always), who were suckered into writing such kind blurbs—and to Melissa Lozada-Oliva, Melissa Broder, J Jennifer Espinoza and Mira Gonzalez, for blurbing the last time. Thank you Sarah Joyce, press photo whisperer. Thank you Julian Montague for the cover illustration featuring the colorful deco decanter of my dreams, and Anuj Mathur for your work on the interior.

Thank you Dylan Baldi for all the kindnesses you share with me each day. Thank you Diane Dupuis, an artist who made me glad to follow into her family biz. Thanks Buster and Lavender, my game changers. Thanks for friendship, support, inspiration, van time clocked, advice, letting me be your fan, et al. to: Audrey Zee Whitesides, Andy Molholt, Devin McKnight, Michael DeForge, Joey Doubek, Sarah Tudzin, Jessi Frick, Lucy Stone, Anna Arboles, Zoë Brecher, Rachel Browne, Michael Falcone, Darl Ferm, Jaclyn Ulman,

Sam Rosenberg, Amar Lal, Ted Leo, Charles Aaron, Liz Phair, Merrick Jarmulowicz, Dara Wier, Peter Gizzi, Mark Leidner, Maryam Qudus, Darcie Wilder, Kristen Arnett, Morgan Parker, Kay Hanley, Miranda Winters, Justin Pizzoferrato, Nick Reinhart, Brett Gregory and Two Dollar Radio, Max Cohen, Jes Skolnik, Chris Richards, Mychal Denzel Smith, Orchid Cugini, Caitlin Bechtel, Faye Orlove, Em Boltz, Colleen Louise Barry, Tony Perez, all of Deerhoof, Sean Cannon, Sarah Gerard, Danniel Schoonebeek, Rob Arnold and Hugo House, Kevin Latimer, Brendan Joyce, Kathy Valentine, Arti Gollapudi, David Catching, Mike Young, Sarah Rose Etter, Cookie Hagendorf, Saskia Hamilton, Johanna Warren, Jamie Loftus, David Bazan, Richard Chiem, Steve Hartlett, Judy Miller Silverman...and any kind friend who has read with me or helped set up a reading. (If I omitted you it was unintentional and due only to the witch's curse that makes me struggle harder with compiling acknowledgments than any other part of the book.)

Thank you to my fellow organizers at UMAW and UMAW Philly. Thank you to the harm reduction groups and advocates who have generously tabled at my bands' shows, passed out resources, and brought their life saving work to nightlife (with emphatic thanks to Kacey Byczek). Thank you to Carpark Records' Todd Hyman, Steph Salas, Alec Moss and Beth Townsend for your support with Wax Nine, and also to the musicians, poets, guest editors and illustrators I've been lucky to publish there—whose visions encourage my own.

Sadie Dupuis is the guitarist, songwriter & singer of rock band Speedy Ortiz, as well as the producer & multi-instrumentalist behind pop project Sad13. Sadie heads the record label Wax Nine, edits its poetry journal, and has written for outlets including *Spin*, *Tape Op* and *NPR*. She holds an MFA in poetry from UMass Amherst, where she also taught writing. *Mouthguard*, her first book, was published in 2018 (Gramma, Black Ocean). Sadie is an organizer with the Union of Musicians and Allied Workers and its Philadelphia local, and has advocated for and consulted on safer spaces measures and harm reduction resources for music venues internationally.